5 Ingredient Cookbook
Family-Friendly Everyday Recipes
with 5 Ingredients or Less
for Busy People on a Budget

by **Vesela Tabakova**

Table Of Contents

3

5 Ingredient Dinner Recipes for Busy Weeknights

For many family cooks, preparing homemade meals after a long strenuous day at work is sometimes hard and even overwhelming. We all have nights when we don't feel like cooking anything complicated or simply don't have the energy to make elaborate meals that no one will eat. With so many commitments these days, convenience usually wins out over healthy most days of the week.

The 5 or less ingredient recipes in my new cookbook will help you get a delicious healthy dinner on the table in an hour or less and will make your hectic day a little less stressful. A good recipe doesn't need a long list of ingredients to make it tasty and while preparing meals at home may seem hard at the beginning, you will soon realize you can throw together a healthy family dinner in the same amount of time you'd need to order a takeout.

Chicken Caprese Salad

Serves: 5-6

Ingredients:

1 lb grape or cherry tomatoes, halved

7 oz Bocconcini - baby mozzarella cheese

4 skinless, boneless chicken breast halves

6-7 fresh basil leaves

6 tbsp olive oil

Directions:

Preheat a grill pan and use half the olive oil to oil the grate. Grill the chicken over high heat, turning once, until cooked through, about 6-7 minutes. Cut it into bite-size pieces.

In a salad bowl, combine the chicken, tomatoes and mozzarella cheese. Sprinkle with basil leaves and season with salt and pepper to taste.

Drizzle olive oil over the salad and serve.

Four Ingredient Chicken Salad

Serves: 5-6

Ingredients:

2 cups shredded chicken

6-7 gherkins, chopped

1/2 cup mayonnaise

1 cup dried cranberries

Directions:

Combine all ingredients in a salad bowl and serve.

Tomato and Blue Cheese Salad

Serves 4

Ingredients:

3-4 large tomatoes, sliced

1 red onion, sliced

2/3 cup crumbled blue cheese

2-3 fresh mint leaves

2 tbsp olive oil

Directions:

Place the tomatoes in a shallow salad bowl. Add the onion and blue cheese. Season with salt to taste.

Drizzle olive oil over the salad and garnish with the fresh mint leaves.

Tomato, Cucumber and Feta Salad

Serves 4

Ingredients:

2 large tomatoes, sliced

1 large cucumber, peeled and sliced

1 red onion, sliced

2/3 cup crumbled feta cheese

2 tbsp olive oil

Directions:

Combine cucumbers, tomatoes, onion, and feta in a large salad bowl.

Drizzle olive oil over the salad and stir to combine.

Mediterranean Cucumber and Yogurt Salad

Serves 4

Ingredients:

2 medium cucumbers, sliced

1 cup plain Greek yogurt or drained yogurt (to taste)

a bunch of fresh dill, finely cut

2 cloves garlic, pressed

1 tbsp white vinegar

Directions:

Spoon yogurt into a salad bowl and mix with vinegar, garlic and dill. Stir in cucumber.

Season with salt and black pepper, to taste and serve.

Fried Zucchinis with Yogurt

Serves 4

Ingredients:

4 zucchinis medium size, washed, peeled and sliced

1 cup all purpose flour

2 cups sunflower oil

2 cups yogurt

2 garlic cloves pressed

Directions:

Wash and peel the zucchinis, and cut them in thin diagonal slices or in rings. Salt and leave them in a suitable bowl placing it inclined to drain away the juices.

Coat the zucchinis with flour, then fry turning on both sides until they are golden-brown (about 3 minutes on each side). Transfer to paper towels and pat dry.

Serve the zucchinis hot or cold, with garlic yogurt on the side.

Potato, Carrot and Green Pea Salad

Serves 5-6

Ingredients:

3 potatoes, peeled, boiled, diced

2 carrots, boiled, diced

1 cup green peas, cooked, drained

1 cup mayonnaise

5 pickled gherkins, chopped

Directions:

Boil the potatoes and carrots, then chop into small cubes.

Put everything, except for the mayonnaise, in a serving bowl and mix. Add salt to taste, then stir in the mayonnaise and set aside for 10-15 minutes. Serve chilled.

Couscous Salad

Serves 4

Ingredients:

2 cups cooked instant couscous

3 ripe tomatoes, diced

3 tbsp olive oil

2 tbsp lemon juice

1 tbsp dried mint

Directions:

In a salad bowl, combine couscous and tomatoes.

In smaller bowl or cup, combine the olive oil, lemon juice and mint, add to the couscous and stir until well combined. Salt to taste and serve.

Green Salad

Serves 4

Ingredients:

one head of lettuce, washed and drained

1 cucumber, peeled and sliced

2 tomatoes, diced

1 bunch of spring onions

3 tbsp sunflower or olive oil

Directions:

Cut the lettuce into thin strips. Slice the cucumber and dice the tomatoes. Chop the spring onions.

Mix all the salad ingredients in a large bowl, add the oil and season with salt to taste.

Beetroot Salad

Serves 4

Ingredients:

2-3 small beets, peeled

3 spring onions, cut

3 cloves garlic, pressed

2 tbsp wine vinegar

2-3 tbsp sunflower oil

Directions:

Place the beats in a steam basket set over a pot of boiling water. Steam for about 12-15 minutes, or until tender. Leave to cool.

Grate the beets and put them in a salad bowl. Add the crushed garlic cloves, the finely cut spring onions and mix well.

Season with salt to taste, vinegar, and sunflower oil.

Carrot Salad

Serves 4

Ingredients:

4 carrots, shredded

1 apple, peeled, cored and shredded

2 garlic cloves, crushed

2 tbsp lemon juice

2 tbsp honey

Directions:

In a bowl, combine the shredded carrots, apple, lemon juice, honey and garlic.

Season with salt and pepper, to taste, toss, and chill before serving.

Stuffed Peppers with Eggs and Feta Cheese

Serves 4

Ingredients:

8 green peppers

3 eggs

2 cups crumbled feta cheese

a bunch of parsley, finely cut

1/3 cup olive oil

Directions:

Remove and discard the tops, seeds, and membranes of the peppers.

With a fork, combine the crumbled feta cheese with 3 beaten eggs and the chopped parsley.

Stuff the peppers with the cheese mixture and arrange them in a baking tray. Drizzle olive oil over them and bake in a preheated to 350 F oven for 30-35 minutes, turning once or twice.

Roasted Eggplant and Pepper Dip

Serves 4

Ingredients:

2 medium eggplants

2 red or green bell peppers

2 tomatoes

3 cloves garlic, crushed

olive oil, as needed

Directions:

Wash and dry the vegetables. Prick the skin of the eggplants. Bake the eggplants, tomatoes and peppers in a pre-heated oven at 420F for about 40 minutes, until the skins are pretty burnt. Take out of the oven and leave in a covered container for about 10 minutes.

Peel the skins off and drain well the extra juices. De-seed the peppers. Cut all the vegetables into small pieces. Add the garlic and blend in a food processor. Add the olive oil and salt to taste. Stir again and serve.

Potato Salad

Serves 5-6

Ingredients:

4-5 large potatoes, peeled and boiled

a bunch of spring onions, finely chopped

1 cup halved black olives

3 tbsp olive oil

fresh parsley, finely cut

Directions:

Peel and boil the potatoes for about 20-25 minutes; drain and leave to cool.

In a salad bowl, add the finely chopped spring onions, olives and olive oil, and mix gently.

Dice the potatoes and add to the salad bowl.

Stir to combine, sprinkle with parsley and serve.

Feta Cheese Stuffed Zucchinis

Serves 5-6

Ingredients:

5-6 zucchinis, peeled

5.5 oz feta cheese, grated

5-6 spring onions, finely cut

3 eggs

½ cup milk

Directions:

Slice the peeled zucchinis lengthwise, hollow and salt.

Combine half of the milk, grated feta cheese, onions and 1 egg in a bowl.

Stuff the zucchinis with the mixture, arrange in a baking dish and pour over the remaining 2 eggs beaten with the rest of the milk. Bake in a preheated to 350 F oven for approximately 30 min.

Turkish Spinach Salad

Serves 1-2

Ingredients:

about 8-9 spinach stems

water to boil the stems

1-2 garlic cloves, crushed

lemon juice or vinegar, to taste

4 tbsp olive oil

Directions:

Trim the stems so that they remain whole. Wash them very well. Steam the spinach stems in a basket over boiling water for 2-3 minutes or until wilted but not too fluffy.

Place the spinach stems on a plate and sprinkle with crushed garlic, olive oil, lemon juice and salt.

White Bean Salad

Serves: 4-5

Ingredients:

1 cup white beans

1 onion

3 tbsp olive oil

3 tbsp white wine vinegar

a bunch of fresh parsley, finely cut

Directions:

Wash the beans and soak them in cold water to swell overnight. Cook in the same water with the peeled onion. When tender, drain and put into a deeper bowl. Remove the onion.

Mix well oil and vinegar; add salt and pepper to taste. Pour over still warm beans, leave to cool about 30-40 minutes.

Chop the onion and the parsley, add to the beans, toss to combine and serve.

Simple Cabbage Salad

Serves 4

Ingredients:

9 oz fresh white cabbage, shredded

9 oz carrots, shredded

½ a bunch of parsley

2 tbsp white vinegar

3 tbsp sunflower oil

Directions:

Combine cabbage and carrots in a salad bowl.

Add in salt to taste, vinegar and oil.

Toss to combine, sprinkle with parsley and serve.

Sausage and Broccoli Pasta Salad

Serves 5-6

Ingredients:

2 cups small pasta

4 oz Italian sausage

2 cups broccoli florets

1 red onion, finely chopped

2 garlic cloves, chopped

2 tbsp mayonnaise

Directions:

In a skillet, cook the sausage for 10-12 min or until cooked through. Add in the onion and garlic and cook for 2-3 minutes, stirring.

Cook the broccoli in boiling water for 3-4 minutes or until tender.

Cook pasta as directed on package. When cooked through but al dente, remove from heat, drain and rinse.

Chop the sausages into pieces and toss with the pasta, broccoli, onion and garlic. Add in mayonnaise.

Toss everything together well with and season with salt and black pepper to taste.

Slow Cooker Onion Dip

Serves 4

Ingredients:

2 cups chopped onions

3 tbsp olive oil

1/2 tsp thyme

8 oz softened cream cheese

1/2 cup mayonnaise

Directions:

Place onions, thyme, olive oil and pinch of salt into a slow cooker. Stir to coat, cover, and cook on high for 6-7 hours, or until onions are well caramelized.

Drain any liquid off the onions and combine with remaining ingredients in a bowl. Season with salt and black pepper to taste.

Slow Cooker Roasted Chickpeas

Serves 4

Ingredients:

2 cups dry chickpeas

water, as needed

1/2 tsp garlic powder

1 tsp paprika

1 tsp cumin

Directions:

In a slow cooker, place the chickpeas and cover with water. Soak overnight then drain and rinse. Cook on low for 8 hours. Drain.

Place chickpeas in the slow cooker and add in all other ingredients. Stir to coat and cook, uncovered, on low for about 10 hours, stirring occasionally.

Tomato Asparagus Frittata

Serves 4

Ingredients:

1 bunch of small asparagus

6 large eggs, whisked

5-6 cherry or grape tomatoes, halved

1 tbsp butter

1/2 tsp garlic powder

Directions:

Preheat the oven to 350 F.

In a skillet, heat butter and gently cook the asparagus for 5 minutes. Add in the tomatoes, eggs and garlic powder then bake for 15 to 20 minutes, or until golden and fluffy.

Cream of Tomato Soup

Serves 5-6

Ingredients:

5 cups chopped fresh tomatoes or 27 oz canned tomatoes, undrained

1 large onion, diced

3 cups water

3 tbsp olive oil

1 tsp sugar

Directions:

Sauté onions in oil in a large soup pot. When onions have softened, add tomatoes and cook until onions are golden and tomatoes soft. Add in water and sugar and simmer 20-30 minutes stirring occasionally.

Blend the soup then return to the pot. Sprinkle with parsley and serve.

Creamy Zucchini Soup

Serves 4

Ingredients:

3 zucchinis, peeled, thinly sliced

1 small onion, finely cut

1 large potato, peeled and chopped

3 cups vegetable broth

1/4 cup fresh basil leaves

Directions:

Heat oil in a saucepan over medium heat and sauté the onion, stirring, for 2-3 minutes or until soft.

Add vegetable broth and bring to the boil, then reduce heat to medium-low. Add in zucchinis and the potato and simmer, stirring occasionally, for 15 minutes, or until the zucchinis are tender.

Add in basil and simmer for 2-3 minutes. Set aside to cool then blend in batches and reheat.

Cream-less Cauliflower Soup

Serves 8

Ingredients:

1 medium head cauliflower, chopped

¼ cup olive oil

1 large onion, finely cut

2-3 garlic cloves, minced

3 cups vegetable broth

Directions:

Heat the olive oil in a large pot over medium heat, and sauté the onion, cauliflower and garlic. Stir in the vegetable broth and bring the mixture to a boil.

Reduce heat, cover, and simmer for 40 minutes.

Remove the soup from heat and blend in a blender or with a hand mixer. Season with salt and pepper to taste and serve.

Mushroom Soup

Serves 4

Ingredients:

1.2 lb mushrooms, peeled and chopped

1 onion, chopped

1 tsp thyme

3 cups vegetable broth

3 tbsp olive oil

Directions:

Sauté onions in a large soup pot until transparent. Add thyme and mushrooms.

Cook for 5 minutes, stirring occasionally, then add the vegetable stock and simmer for another 15-20 minuets. Blend, season and serve.

Creamy Egg and Onion Scramble

Serves 4

Ingredients:

1 large onion, finely cut

2 tbsp sour cream

8 eggs

2 tbsp olive oil

2 tbsp fresh parsley, finely cut, to serve

Directions:

In a large pan, sauté the onion in olive oil, over medium heat, stirring, about 10 min.

Add the eggs and cook for 1-2 minutes. Add the sour cream, stir, and cook until well mixed and not too liquid.

Stir in the parsley and serve.

Salami Scrambled Eggs

Serves 5-6

Ingredients:

1 small onion, finely cut

1 cup thickly sliced salami, cut into 1/4-inch strips

2 cups baby rocket leaves, torn

8 eggs

4 tbsp olive oil

Directions:

In a large pan sauté onion over medium heat, till transparent. Reduce heat and add the salami strips. Cook, stirring occasionally, until lightly browned, about 2 minutes.

Add the rocket leaves and all eggs, stir, and cook until the eggs are softly set.

Season with salt and black pepper and remove from heat.

Italian Sausage and Green Beans

Serves 5-6

Ingredients:

1 lb bulk Italian sausage

1 cup cooked small pasta

1 bag (12 oz) frozen cut green beans, thawed

1 large tomato, diced

1 tbsp tomato paste

Directions:

In a skillet, cook sausage over medium-high heat 5-6 minutes, stirring frequently, until no longer pink. Drain excess fat.

Stir in pasta, green beans, tomato and tomato paste.

Season with salt and black pepper and simmer about 15 minutes, stirring occasionally, until beans are tender.

Peanut Butter Dump Chicken

Serves 4

Ingredients:

4-5 chicken breast halves, cut in 1 inch pieces

3-4 green onions, finely cut

4-5 white button mushrooms, sliced

¾ cup smooth peanut butter

1 tbsp soy sauce

Directions:

Preheat oven to 350 F.

Spray a casserole with non stick spray.

Place all ingredients into the casserole and turn chicken to coat.

Bake for about 40 minutes or until chicken juices run clear.

Crock Pot Chicken and Leek Drumsticks

Serves 4

Ingredients:

8 chicken drumsticks

6-7 leeks, trimmed, thinly sliced

4-5 white button mushrooms, sliced

1 cup heavy cream

1 tbsp chopped fresh tarragon

Directions:

Spray the slow cooker with non stick spray.

Place all ingredients into slow cooker and turn drumsticks to coat well.

Cook on low for 6-7 hours.

Chicken and Potato Casserole

Serves 4

Ingredients:

4 skinless, boneless chicken breast halves

2 lbs baby potatoes

1 cup water

3 tbsp olive oil

1 tbsp dried oregano

Directions:

Preheat the oven to 350 F. Heat oil in a non stick frying pan over medium heat. Cook half the chicken, turning occasionally, for 5 minutes, or until brown all over. Set aside. Repeat with remaining chicken.

Peel the potatoes and cut into quarters, lengthwise. Transfer the chicken to an ovenproof dish and add the potatoes on and around it. Sprinkle with dried oregano and water and season with salt and black pepper, to taste.

Roast uncovered at 350 F for 40 minutes. Halfway through stir gently. If needed, add a little more water.

Easy Chicken Parmigiana

Serves 4

Ingredients:

4 chicken breast fillets

1 eggplant, peeled and sliced lengthwise

1 can tomatoes, diced

9 oz mozzarella cheese, sliced

2 tbsp olive oil

Directions:

In an ovenproof casserole, heat olive oil and brown the chicken pieces.

Place the eggplant slices over the chicken and add in tomatoes. Top with mozzarella slices and bake in a preheated to 350 F for 20 minutes or until the cheese is golden.

Honey Mustard Chicken with Parsnips

Serves 5-6

Ingredients:

7-8 chicken tights

1 lb parsnips, peeled and cut into sticks

3 tbsp olive oil

5 tbsp mustard

3 tbsp honey

Directions:

In a bowl, combine mustard and honey.

Heat olive oil in an ovenproof casserole dish and brown the chicken. Add in parsnips and sauté for a minute, stirring.

Stir in honey mixture, season with salt and pepper to taste, cover, and simmer for 30 minutes.

Mediterranean Chicken Drumstick Casserole

Serves 4

Ingredients

8 chicken drumsticks

2 leeks, trimmed, thinly sliced

1 cup canned tomatoes

1 tsp Italian seasoning

1 cup canned chickpeas, drained and rinsed

Directions:

Preheat the oven to 350 F. Heat the oil in a non stick frying pan over medium heat. Add half the chicken and cook, turning occasionally, for 5 minutes, or until brown all over. Transfer chicken to a big baking dish. Repeat with the remaining chicken.

Add the leek to the pan and cook, stirring, for 3-5 minutes or until soft. Add in tomatoes, chickpeas, and Italian seasoning and bring to the boil. Remove from heat. Pour over the chicken.

Bake in a preheated to 350 F oven for 40 minutes or until the chicken is tender. Season with salt and pepper to taste.

Pesto Chicken

Serves 4

Ingredients:

5-6 chicken breast halves

1 small jar pesto sauce

1 cup sour cream

non-stick spray

Directions:

In a bowl, combine pesto and sour cream.

Heat oven to 350 degrees F. Spray a casserole with non stick spray. Place chicken and pesto mixture into it, turn chicken to coat.

Bake for 35-40 minutes or until chicken juices run clear.

Herbal Lamb Stew

Serves 4

Ingredients:

1 lb lamb, cubed

4 cups fresh spring onions, chopped

3 cups fresh parsley, finely cut

2 tbsp butter

1 pinch saffron (6-8 strands)

Directions:

In a medium pot, add the lamb, onions, and enough cold water to just cover. Bring to the boil over high heat, then reduce to a simmer. Cook until the lamb is tender, about 90 minutes.

Pour out all but 1/2 cup of the broth in the pot (save the remainder for another use if needed), and stir in the saffron. Turn off the heat.

Heat butter in a deep casserole. Gently stew parsley for about 5 minutes, stirring, until wilted.

Add the lamb with the broth and cook, stirring occasionally, for 10 minutes. Season with with salt and pepper and serve.

Beef and Okra Stew

Serves 6

Ingredients:

1 lb stewing beef

2 lbs frozen okra

1 onion, chopped

1 cup canned tomatoes, diced

4 tbsp olive oil

Directions:

In a large saucepan, heat olive oil and seal meat. Add in onions and sauté, stirring for 2-3 minutes.

Add tomatoes and salt and pepper to taste. Stir and combine well.

Add in okra and bring to a boil, then reduce heat to low and simmer, covered, for an hour or until meat is tender and done.

Uncover and simmer for five more minutes.

Easy Beef Crock Pot

Serves 4-5

Ingredients:

2 lbs beef, cubed

1 small onion, finely cut

1 celery rib, finely cut

1 can cream of mushrooms soup

½ cup water or vegetable broth

Directions:

Spray the slow cooker with non stick spray.

Combine all ingredients into the slow cooker, cover, and cook on low for 7-9 hours.

Pork and Mushroom Crock Pot

Serves 4

Ingredients:

2 lbs pork tenderloin, sliced

2 cups chopped white button mushrooms

1 can cream of mushroom soup

½ cup sour cream

1/2 cup chopped parsley, finely cut

Directions:

Spray the slow cooker with non stick spray.

Combine all ingredients into the slow cooker. Cover, and cook on low for 7-9 hours.

Tuscan Baked Fish

Serves 4

Ingredients:

4 boneless, skinless fish fillets- cod, tilapia, or another flaky white fish

1 can diced tomatoes with basil

1/2 onion, diced

3 tbsp olive oil

3 tbsp capers

Directions:

Preheat oven to 350 F. Heat olive oil in an ovenproof casserole and sauté onion until translucent. Add in tomatoes and capers. Stir and cook for 4-5 minutes. Add fish.

Bake for 15-20 minutes in the preheated oven, until fish is easily flaked with a fork.

Easy Baked Salmon

Serves 4

Ingredients:

1 salmon fillet

4 tbsp butter, melted

6-7 garlic cloves, crushed

3 tbsp lemon juice

1/3 cup finely cut dill

Directions:

Preheat oven to 350 F. Line a casserole with aluminum foil. Place the salmon in the middle of the foil.

In a cup, combine melted butter, lemon juice, garlic, and dill. Whisk together.

Pour butter mixture over salmon, pull the sides and ends of the aluminum foil up, and pinch together, covering the salmon completely.

Bake for 15-20 minutes in the preheated oven, until fish is easily flaked with a fork.

Brussels Sprouts Egg and Tomato Skillet

Serves: 2

Ingredients:

1 lb Brussels Sprouts, halved

3-4 spring onions, chopped

6 cherry tomatoes, halved

4 eggs

2 tbsp olive oil

Directions:

In an cast iron skillet, heat olive oil over medium heat. Gently sauté spring onions for 1-2 minutes.

Add in Brussels sprouts and cherry tomatoes and season with salt. Cook for 5 minutes then crack the eggs.

Cook until egg whites have set.

Poached Eggs on Avocado and Feta Toast

Serves: 4

Ingredients:

1 avocado, peeled and chopped

½ cup feta cheese, crumbled

4 slices crusty white bread, lightly toasted

1 tomato, sliced

4 eggs

Directions:

Fill a large saucepan with water and bring to a hard boil over high heat. Once boiling, reduce the heat so the water is simmering and crack in the eggs. Cook for 2 1/2 minutes.

Mash the avocado with a fork until smooth. Combine with feta cheese.

Toast 4 slices of white bread until golden. Spoon 1/4 of the avocado mixture onto each slice of bread. Top with tomatoes and put a poached egg on top. Season with salt and pepper to taste, and serve.

Hummus Zucchini Toast

Serves: 2

Ingredients:

4 tbsp hummus

4 tbsp shaved zucchini

2 tbsp roasted salted sunflower seeds

2 slices crusty white bread, lightly toasted

Directions:

Toast 4 slices of white bread until golden.

Spread hummus onto each slice of bread; top with zucchini and sunflower seeds. Season with salt and pepper to taste, and serve.

Green Pea Stew

Serves 4

Ingredients:

1 large can green peas or a 1 bag frozen green peas

4 tbsp olive oil

1 tsp paprika

½ bunch of fresh dill

4 cloves garlic, chopped

Directions:

In a soup pot, heat the olive oil and gently sauté the garlic and green peas. Add in a little warm water and simmer for 20 minutes, stirring occasionally.

Season with salt and black pepper to taste, sprinkle with the finely cut dill, and serve.

Easy Leek Stew

Serves 5-6

Ingredients:

1 lb leeks, cut

fresh, ground pepper to taste

4 tbsp sunflower oil

1/2 cup vegetable broth

2 tbsp tomato paste

Directions:

Carefully clean leeks; cut off the stemmy bottoms and the dark green leaves, leave only white and light green parts. Cut leeks lengthwise in quarters, then into about 1 inch squares.

Heat oil in a heavy wide saucepan or sauté pan; add leeks, salt, pepper, and stir over low heat for 5 minutes. Add in vegetable broth and bring to boil, cover and simmer over low heat, stirring often, for about 10 to 15 minutes or until leeks are tender.

Add in tomato paste, raise heat to medium, uncover and let juices reduce to about half.

Cheesy Potato and Leek Stew

Serves 4-5

Ingredients:

2-3 leek stems cut into thick rings

12 oz potatoes

1 carrot, chopped

5 tbsp olive oil

1 cup grated Parmesan cheese

Directions:

Peel the potatoes, wash them and cut them into small cubes. Slice the leeks and chop the carrot. Put the potatoes, carrot and leeks in a pot along with some water and the oil. The water should cover the vegetables.

Season with salt to taste and bring to boil. Simmer until tender. Sprinkle with Parmesan cheese and serve.

Spinach with Rice

Serves 4

Ingredients:

1.5 lb fresh spinach, washed, drained and chopped

1/2 cup rice

1 onion

5 tbsp olive oil

2 cups water

Directions:

Heat the oil in a large skillet and cook the onions until soft. Add the washed and drained rice and stir to combine.

Add two cups of warm water stirring constantly as the rice absorbs it, and simmer for 10 more minutes.

Wash the spinach well and cut it in strips then add to the rice and cook until it wilts. Remove from the heat and season to taste with salt and black pepper.

Rice with Leeks and Olives

Serves 4-6

Ingredients:

6 large leeks, cleaned and sliced into bite sized pieces (about 6-7 cups of sliced leeks)

20 black olives pitted, chopped

1/4 cup olive oil

1 cup rice

2 1/2 cups warm water

Directions:

In a large saucepan, sauté the leeks in the olive oil for 4-5 minutes. Cut and add the olives and 1/2 cup water. Bring temperature down, cover saucepan and cook for 10 minutes, stirring occasionally.

Add rice and 2 cups of hot water, bring to boil, cover and simmer for 15 more minutes, stirring occasionally.

Remove from heat and allow to 'sit' for 30 minutes before serving so that the rice can absorb any liquid left.

New Potatoes with Herbs

Serves 4-5

Ingredients:

2.25 oz small new potatoes

1/2 cup olive oil

1/2 cup water

2 tbsp Italian seasoning

1/2 cup finely cut dill

Directions:

Wash the young potatoes, cut them in halves if too big, and put them in a baking dish. Pour the olive oil and water over the potatoes.

Season with the Italian seasoning, salt and pepper. Bake for 30-40 minutes at 350F and serve sprinkled with fresh dill.

Paprika Rice

Serves 6-7

Ingredients:

1 cup rice, rinsed

2 red peppers, cut

1 can tomatoes, undrained and diced

1 tbsp paprika

3 tbsp olive oil

Directions:

In a large saucepan, heat olive oil and gently sauté the peppers for 1-2 minutes until fragrant. Add in paprika and rice and cook, stirring constantly until the rice becomes transparent.

Add in 2 cups of hot water and the canned tomatoes. Stir, and season with salt and pepper.

Simmer over medium heat for about 20 minutes.

Roasted Broccoli

Serves 4

Ingredients:

2 medium broccoli heads, cut into florets

4 garlic cloves, lightly crushed

1 tsp fresh rosemary

1/4 cup olive oil

1 cup grated Parmesan cheese

Directions:

In a deep bowl, combine olive oil, rosemary, garlic and Parmesan cheese together. Toss in broccoli and coat well.

Place in a baking dish in one layer and roast in a preheated to 350 F oven for 20 minutes; stir and bake for 10 minutes more.

Poached Eggs with Feta and Yogurt

Serves 4

Ingredients:

8 eggs

2 cups plain yogurt

10 oz feta cheese, crumbled

2 tsp paprika

2 oz butter

Directions:

Combine the yogurt and the grated cheese. Divide the mixture into four plates.

Poach the eggs, take them out with a serving spoon and place two eggs on top of the yogurt mixture in each plate.

Brown the butter together with paprika and pour one quarter over each plate before serving.

Beet Fries

Serves: 4

Ingredients:

3 beets, cut in strips

3 tbsp olive oil

1 cup finely cut spring onions

2 garlic cloves, crushed

3 tbsp grated Parmesan cheese

Directions:

Line a baking dish with baking paper. Wash and peel the beets then cut them in strips similar to French fries. Toss the beets with olive oil, spring onions, garlic and Parmesan cheese.

Arrange beets on a prepared baking sheet and place in a preheated to 425 F oven for 25-30 minutes, flipping halfway through.

Roasted Artichoke Hearts

Serves: 4

Ingredients:

3 cans artichoke hearts

3-4 garlic cloves, pressed

4 tsp olive oil

1 tbsp Italian seasoning

2-3 tbsp lemon juice, to serve

Directions:

Preheat oven to 375 F. Drain the artichoke hearts and rinse them with water.

Combine garlic, olive oil and Italian seasoning. Toss the artichoke hearts in that mixture.

Arrange the artichoke hearts in a lined baking dish and bake for about 40 minutes stirring a few times.

Season with salt and pepper to taste and serve with lemon juice.

Potatoes Baked in Milk

Serves 5-6

Ingredients:

4-5 medium potatoes, peeled and sliced

1 cup milk

5 tbsp olive oil

1 tsp paprika

1 tsp summer savory

Directions:

Wash the potatoes, peel them and cut them in thin slices.

Put in a large baking dish together with the milk, oil, salt, pepper, paprika and savory.

Combine everything very well. Bake for about 30 minutes at 350 F.

Cheesy Potato and Zucchini Bake

Serves 6

Ingredients:

1 lb potatoes, peeled and sliced into rounds

3 zucchinis, sliced into rounds

1 can tomatoes, pureed

1 tsp Italian seasoning

1/2 cup grated Parmesan cheese

Directions:

Place the potatoes and zucchinis in a large, shallow ovenproof baking dish. Pour over the the pureed tomatoes. Sprinkle with the Italian seasoning and toss the everything together. Top with Parmesan cheese.

Bake in the preheated to 350 F oven for 40 minutes.

Crispy Feta Cheese Pastry

Serves 6

Ingredients:

14 oz filo pastry

5 eggs

½ cup yogurt

8 oz feta cheese

3.5 oz butter

Directions:

Preheat the oven to 350 F. Combine the eggs, cheese and yogurt in a bowl. Melt the butter in a bowl.

Grease the base of a baking tray, at least 1.5 inch deep, with some of the butter. Take the filo sheets and lay them on a dry surface.

Place one sheet of filo pastry in the baking tray. Brush with melted butter using a pastry brush. Lay another sheet of pastry on top and brush with butter. Sprinkle some of the cheese mixture evenly over the butter-basted pastry. Continue alternating two sheets of butter-basted pastry with the cheese mixture. Repeat for 6 or 7 layers until all the sheets of pastry have been used up or the pie reaches the top of the baking tray, but make sure you finish with a sheet of pastry on top.

If there is any mixture left over brush the top of the Cheese Pastry in the tray, if there is none left - brush some butter.

Place the tray in the oven and bake for 20 minutes until slightly risen and golden. Serve warm.

French Toast

Serves 4

Ingredients:

8 slices stale bread

4 eggs, beaten

2/3 cup milk

1/2 cup sunflower oil

Directions:

Slice the bread into thin 1/2 inch slices. Dip first in milk, then in the beaten eggs.

Fry in hot oil. Serve hot, sprinkled with sugar, honey, jam, feta cheese or whatever topping you prefer.

Peanut Butter and Banana On Toast

Serves 1

Ingredients:

2 slices white bread

1 large banana

1 tsp orange zest

2 tbsp crunchy peanut butter

Directions:

Toast bread and slice banana.

Layer banana on one slice of toast. Spread the second slice with peanut butter, Sprinkle with orange zest, then sandwich the two together and eat straight away.

Cinnamon and Sugar Peanuts

Serves 4

Ingredients:

12 oz unsalted, roasted peanuts

1 tbsp melted butter

3 tsp ground cinnamon

⅓ cup brown sugar

Directions:

Place the peanuts, cinnamon and sugar in a slow cooker. Drizzle with butter, stir and cook on low, uncovered, for 3 hours, stirring occasionally.

Spread the peanuts onto a cookie sheet or parchment paper until cool and dry.

FREE BONUS RECIPES: 10 Ridiculously Easy Jam and Jelly Recipes Anyone Can Make

A Different Strawberry Jam

Makes 6-7 11 oz jars

Ingredients:

4 lb fresh small strawberries (stemmed and cleaned)

5 cups sugar

1 cup water

2 tbsp lemon juice or 1 tsp citric acid

Directions:

Mix water and sugar and bring to the boil. Simmer sugar syrup for 5-6 minutes then slowly drop in the cleaned strawberries. Stir and bring to the boil again. Lower heat and simmer, stirring and skimming any foam off the top once or twice. Drop a small amount of the jam on a plate and wait a minute to see if it has thickened. If it has gelled enough, turn off the heat. If not, keep boiling and test every 5 minutes until ready. Two or three minutes before you remove the jam from the heat, add lemon juice or citric acid and stir well.

Ladle the hot jam in the jars until 1/8-inch from the top. Place the lid on top and flip the jar upside down. Continue until all of the jars are filled and upside down. Allow the jam to cool completely before turning right-side up. Press on the lid to check and see if it has sealed. If one of the jars lids doesn't pop up- the jar is not sealed–store it in a refrigerator.

Raspberry Jam

Makes 4-5 11 oz jars

Ingredients:

4 cups raspberries

4 cups sugar

1 tsp vanilla extract

1/2 tsp citric acid

Directions:

Gently wash and drain the raspberries. Lightly crush them with a potato masher, food mill or a food processor. Do not puree, it is better to have bits of fruit. Sieve half of the raspberry pulp to remove some of the seeds. Combine sugar and raspberries in a wide, thick-bottomed pot and bring mixture to a full rolling boil, stirring constantly. Skim any scum or foam that rises to the surface. Boil until the jam sets.

Test by putting a small drop on a cold plate – if the jam is set, it will wrinkle when given a small poke with your finger. Add citric acid, vanilla, and stir. Simmer for 2-3 minutes more, then ladle into hot jars. Flip upside down or process 10 minutes in boiling water.

Raspberry-Peach Jam

Makes 4-5 11 oz jars

Ingredients:

2 lb peaches

1 1/2 cup raspberries

4 cups sugar

1 tsp citric acid

Directions:

Wash and slice the peaches. Clean the raspberries and combine them with the peaches is a wide, heavy-bottomed saucepan. Cover with sugar and set aside for a few hours or overnight. Bring the fruit and sugar to a boil over medium heat, stirring occasionally. Remove any foam that rises to the surface.

Boil until the jam sets. Add citric acid and stir. Simmer for 2-3 minutes more, then ladle into hot jars. Flip upside down or process 10 minutes in boiling water.

Blueberry Jam

Makes 4-5 11 oz jars

Ingredients:

4 cups granulated sugar

3 cups blueberries (frozen and thawed or fresh)

3/4 cup honey

2 tbsp lemon juice

1 tsp lemon zest

Directions:

Gently wash and drain the blueberries. Lightly crush them with a potato masher, food mill or a food processor. Add the honey, lemon juice, and lemon zest, then bring to a boil over medium-high heat. Boils for 10-15 minutes, stirring from time to time. Boil until the jam sets.

Test by putting a small drop on a cold plate – if the jam is set, it will wrinkle when given a small poke with your finger. Skim off any foam, then ladle the jam into jars. Seal, flip upside down or process for 10 minutes in boiling water.

Triple Berry Jam

Makes 4-5 11 oz jars

Ingredients:

1 cup strawberries

1 cup raspberries

2 cups blueberries

4 cups sugar

1 tsp citric acid

Directions:

Mix berries and add sugar. Set aside for a few hours or overnight. Bring the fruit and sugar to the boil over medium heat, stirring frequently. Remove any foam that rises to the surface. Boil until the jam sets. Add citric acid, salt and stir.

Simmer for 2-3 minutes more, then ladle into hot jars. Flip upside down or process 10 minutes in boiling water.

Red Currant Jelly

Makes 6-7 11 oz jars

Ingredients:

2 lb fresh red currants

1/2 cup water

3 cups sugar

1 tsp citric acid

Directions:

Place the currants into a large pot, and crush with a potato masher or berry crusher. Add in water, and bring to a boil. Simmer for 10 minutes. Strain the fruit through a jelly or cheese cloth and measure out 4 cups of the juice.

Pour the juice into a large saucepan, and stir in the sugar. Bring to full rolling boil, then simmer for 20-30 minutes, removing any foam that may rise to the surface. When the jelly sets, ladle in hot jars, flip upside down or process in boiling water for 10 minutes.

White Cherry Jam

Makes 3-4 11 oz jars

Ingredients:

2 lb cherries

3 cups sugar

2 cups water

1 tsp citric acid

Directions:

Wash and stone cherries. Combine water and sugar and bring to the boil. Boil for 5-6 minutes then remove from heat and add cherries. Bring to a rolling boil and cook until set. Add citric acid, stir and boil 1-2 minutes more.

Ladle in hot jars, flip upside down or process in boiling water for 10 minutes.

Cherry Jam

Makes 3-4 11 oz jars

Ingredients:

2 lb fresh cherries, pitted, halved

4 cups sugar

1/2 cup lemon juice

Directions:

Place the cherries in a large saucepan. Add sugar and set aside for an hour. Add the lemon juice and place over low heat. Cook, stirring occasionally, for 10 minutes or until sugar dissolves. Increase heat to high and bring to a rolling boil.

Cook for 5-6 minutes or until jam is set. Remove from heat and ladle hot jam into jars, seal and flip upside down.

Oven Baked Ripe Fig Jam

Makes 3-4 11 oz jars

Ingredients:

2 lb ripe figs

2 cups sugar

1 ½ cups water

2 tbsp lemon juice

Directions:

Arrange the figs in a Dutch oven, if they are very big, cut them in halves. Add sugar and water and stir well. Bake at 350 F for about one and a half hours. Do not stir. You can check the readiness by dropping a drop of the syrup in a cup of cold water – if it falls to the bottom without dissolving, the jam is ready. If the drop dissolves before falling, you can bake it a little longer. Take out of the oven, add lemon juice and ladle in the warm jars. Place the lids on top and flip the jars upside down. Allow the jam to cool completely before turning right-side up.

If you want to process the jams - place them into a large pot, cover the jars with water by at least 2 inches and bring to a boil. Boil for 10 minutes, remove the jars and sit to cool.

Quince Jam

Makes 5-6 11 oz jars

Ingredients:

4 lb quinces

5 cups sugar

2 cups water

1 tsp lemon zest

3 tbsp lemon juice

Directions:

Combine water and sugar in a deep, thick-bottomed saucepan and bring it to the boil. Simmer, stirring until the sugar has completely dissolved. Rinse the quinces, cut in half, and discard the cores. Grate the quinces, using a cheese grater or a blender to make it faster. Quince flesh tends to darken very quickly, so it is good to do this as fast as possible.

Add the grated quinces to the sugar syrup and cook uncovered, stirring occasionally until the jam turns pink and thickens to desired consistency, about 40 minutes. Drop a small amount of the jam on a plate and wait a minute to see if it has thickened. If it has gelled enough, turn off the heat. If not, keep boiling and test every 2-3 minutes until ready. Two or three minutes before you remove the jam from the heat, add lemon juice and lemon zest and stir well.

Ladle in hot, sterilized jars and flip upside down.

Before You Go

Thank you for purchasing my book and trying out my recipes! If you enjoyed my 5 ingredient meals, please consider leaving a review at Amazon, even if it's only a line or two; it would be really appreciated.

About the Author

Vesela lives in Bulgaria with her family of six (including the Jack Russell Terrier). Her passion is going green in everyday life and she loves to prepare homemade cosmetic and beauty products for all her family and friends.

Vesela has been publishing her cookbooks for over a year now. If you want to see other healthy family recipes that she has published, together with some natural beauty books, you can check out her Author Page on Amazon.

Printed in Great Britain
by Amazon